SAINT PETERSBURG

PETERHOF · TSARSKOYE SELO · PAVLOVSK

IVAN FIODOROV ART PUBLISHERS
SAINT PETERSBURG
2003

Text by Abram Raskin

Translated from the Russian by Valery Fateyev

Design by Nikolai Kutovoi

Colour correction by Liubov Kornilova

Computer layout by Yelena Morozova

Photographs by

Sergei Alexeyev, Valentin Baranovsky, Leonid Bogdanov, Pavel Demidov, Vladimir Denisov,

Konstantin Doka, Natalia Doka, Vladimir Dorokhov, Sergei Falin, Leonid Gerkus, Grigory Khatin,

Leonard Kheifets, Arthur Kirakozov, Romuald Kirillov, Vladimir Melnikov, Yury Molodkovets,

Victor Savik, Georgy Shablovsky, Yevgeny Siniaver, Alexander Sladkov, Vladimir Terebenin,

Oleg Trubsky, Vasily Vorontsov and Alexander Yaroslavtsev

Edited by Maria Lyzhenkova

Managing editor Sergei Vesnin

ISBN 5-93893-021-9 (Softcover edition)
ISBN 5-93893-031-6 (Hardcover edition)

Saint Petersburg, the city symbolizing Russia's European aspect, ranks with the great capitals of the world. The very name of the city suggests its international character. Unlike the names of other European capitals, it consists of two meaningful words. The Russian version of the name combines elements of different languages: its first part derives from the Latin word for "saint", followed by the Apostle's name, Peter, which means "rock" in Greek, and "burg", a city in German or Dutch. Therefore the name of the young capital implies, in its symbolism, a reference to Tsar Peter the Great and his holy patron, and cultural links with Ancient Greece and Rome, as well as with Germany and Holland.

The name of St Petersburg emphasizes, in a symbolic form, the city's link with Catholic Rome whose patron the Apostle Peter was. Even the emblem of St Petersburg, which includes two crossing anchors, is strikingly similar to that of Vatican.

The main stages in the history of the second Russian capital can be traced in its architecture. The peri-ods of outstanding reigns and major architectural landmarks of the eighteenth to twentieth centuries are inseparable and form together an integral chronicle of St Petersburg.

The city was founded on Hare Island by the will of Peter the Great on 27 May 1703, the Church Feast dedicated to the name of the Holy Trinity. The monarch's ideas were perfectly realized by the Italian architect Domenico Trezzini, the supervisor of construction work at its initial stage, who was active in the city from 1703 to 1734. Peter the Great ordered to invite to Russia skilled and experienced foreign architects who distinguished themselves in their own countries. Among them were those who evolved a distinctive style of the age known as the Petrine Baroque — Jean-Baptiste Le Blond, Mario-Giovanni Fontana, Johann Friedrich Schädel, Georg Johann Mattarnovi, Andreas Schlüter and Niccolo Michetti, as well as the sculptor and architect Bartolomeo Carlo Rastrelli. The memory of the founder of the city is personified in the monument created by the outstanding sculptor Etienne Maurice Falconet in 1768.

Construction work in the city on the Neva was suspended between 1728 and 1732, when the capital was shifted back to Moscow by the subsequent short-lived monarchs who preferred it as the royal residence. After Empress Anna Ioannovna had returned to St Petersburg, however, the newly built city regained its role as the capital of Russia and construction work was revived. The years 1732–40 saw the fulfillment of numerous construction projects which shaped the city's general architectural appearance and layout for centuries to come. The leading figures responsible for this work were the engineer Burchard Christoph Minich and the architect Piotr Yeropkin. The reign of Empress Elizabeth Petrovna was marked by the flowering of the St Petersburg Baroque. Outstanding examples of this expressive style were created by Bartolomeo Francesco Rastrelli and Savva Chevakinsky.

The reign of Catherine the Great (1762–96) saw the fast development and predominance of the style of Classicism. The 1760s and 1770s are described in the history of St Petersburg architecture as

the period of early Classicism, with Jean-Baptiste Vallin de La Mothe, Antonio Rinaldi and Yury Velten as its main representatives. The period from the 1780s to the 1800s was dominated by mature or austere Classicism. Its leading architects were Ivan Starov and Giacomo Quarenghi. The distinctive features of High Classicism (1800–30) can be seen in architectural works by Jean François Thomas de Thomon, Andrei Voronikhin and Andreyan Zakharov. An exclusive role in the creation of the ensembles of "classical" St Petersburg belongs to Carlo Rossi. A major figure of High Classicism was Vasily Stasov. The best achievements of St Petersburg architecture in the middle and second half of the nineteenth century are associated with Auguste de Montferrand and Andrei Stakenschneider.

In the second half of the nineteenth century the former stylistic unity was replaced by all sorts of experiments and imitations.

The late nineteenth and early twentieth centuries saw a marked change in the appearance of St Petersburg owing to the introduction of buildings in the Art Nouveau style, with Fiodor Lidval as a leading figure of the trend.

The radical changes in the social and economic system of the state which took place in 1917 led the development of St Petersburg architecture along new lines. But the architects of the city, never forgetting the creative traditions of the past managed to preserve the integral and graceful look of the Northern capital.

←

Decembrists' (Senate or Peter's) Square

The Neva. The Palace Bridge

*The Stock Exchange.
The display and interior of the
Naval Museum*

*The Spit of Vasilyevsky Island.
The Stock Exchange*

*The Rostral Column.
Allegorical sculpture:*
The Volkhov River

The eastern tip of Vasilyevsky Island
known as its "spit" divides a branch from
the mainstream of the Neva with its
majestic flow and sense of expanse.
For a long time the Spit of Vasilyevsky
Island was used a the main trade port.
That is why this site was chosen for
the building of the Stock Exchange.
In 1805–16, Thomas de Thomon designed
an architectural complex including the
buildings of the Stock Exchange, the
Rostral Columns and a granite embankment. The predominant structure of the
ensemble was the Stock Exchange. Its
composition and decor imitate the temples
of Ancient Greece and Rome. Similar to
ancient temples, the main volume was
skirted with forty-four Doric columns
spaced along its perimeter. Above them
were placed sculptural groups personifying the prosperity of the Russian Navy
and Trade. They were carved of Pudost
stone after models by Ivan Prokofyev and
Feodosy Shchedrin by the famous master
stone-cutter Samson Sukhanov.
From 1940 the building of the Stock
Exchange houses the Central Naval
Museum. The square is decorated with
two Rostral Columns, almost 32 metres

high (with lamps). The tradition comes
from Ancient Greece and Rome where
rostral columns used to be erected to
commemorate naval victories and the
shafts of the columns were adorned
with *rostra* or prows of captured ships.
On the granite pediments at the feet of the
St Petersburg columns are placed seated
stone figures personifying the rivers Volga,
Neva, Volkhov (by Philippe Thiébot) and
the Dnieper (by Joseph Camberlain).
The sculptural decor of the columns
is enhanced by twenty-eight decorative

rostra of sheet copper. The granite sheathing of the banks serves as a monumental "setting" of the ensemble of the Spit. The Stock Exchange, the focus of the ensemble, is perceived in the panoramic view of the Neva as a powerful chord of the organ matching the austere spirit of Northern Palmyra.

Panoramic view of the Spit of Vasilyevsky Island and the Peter and Paul Fortress

Panoramic view of the Peter and Paul Fortress

Stretching along the right bank of the Neva is an island occupied by the ensemble of the Peter and Paul Fortress. The Kronwerk Stream separates the fortress from the Petrograd Side (formerly Birch or City Island) and the branches of the Neva divide it from Vasilyevsky Island. It was Peter the Great who chose this island as a site for building a citadel. The fortress became the kernel of the new Russian city. On 29 June 1703, 32 days after the foundation of the fortress, on the feast day of the SS Apostles Peter and Paul, a wooden church was founded on the island, and on 8 July 1712 the construction of a stone cathedral began (the wooden church was preserved within it until 1719).

The fortress was named after the cathedral, the Peter and Paul Fortress. It contains six bastions, six curtain walls (the walls linking the bastions) and six gates. The main gate, known as the Peter Gate, is decorated with allegorical sculpture, bas-reliefs and the emblem of Russia.

In 1703–04 the fortifications and structures were built of earth and wood. The years 1706–40 saw the stone and brick period of construction. In 1779–85 the walls were faced with granite. The SS Peter and Paul Cathedral, consecrated on 27 June 1732, is the dominant feature of the fortress. Its bell-tower supports a tall spire crowned with the Angel carrying a cross and blessing the city. The overall height of the spire is 122.5 metres.

The important decorative feature of the cathedral is its unique carved iconostasis with the cast Holy Gate and a carved lectern decorated with sculpture, produced in Moscow to the drawings of Domenico Trezzini by the architect and carver Ivan Zarudny together with his assistants Ivan Telega and Trifon Ivanov, as well as by some other Moscow carvers. The SS Peter and Paul Cathedral served as a burial place of the Russian Emperors and members of the royal family. There are thirty-two tombs there beginning with that of Peter the Great. By 1908 the Grand Ducal Burial Vault was put up next to the cathedral. Built to the design of David Grimm, with the participation

The SS Peter and Paul Cathedral. The Boat House

Angel on the spire of the SS Peter and Paul Cathedral

The SS Peter and Paul Cathedral. Interior

The SS Peter and Paul Cathedral. The lectern

The Catherine Chapel of the SS Peter and Paul Cathedral
Tomb of Emperor Nicholas II, Empress Alexandra Feodorovna and their children

The SS Peter and Paul Cathedral. Iconostasis. Detail of the Holy Gate

Tomb of Peter the Great

of Osip Tomishko and Leonty Benois, it was consecrated to St Alexander Nevsky. Before 1917 there were thirteen burials of the Romanov house there. In 1992, Grand Duke Vladimir, the great-grandson of Alexander II, was interred in the Burial Vault. Three years later the remains of his parents, Grand Duke Kirill Vladimirovich and his consort, were buried there.

In 1998 the burial of the remains of Nicholas II, his wife, their children, the family's doctor and three servants shot in 1918 took place.

The ensemble of the Peter and Paul Fortress is the only monument in St Petersburg which covers its entire history.

The Neva is a "cradle" of St Petersburg, which not only predetermined its emergence as a port vital for Russia, but became the focal element in the spatial layout of the city never losing its significance to the present day. It was along the banks of the Neva, stretching within the city for about 24 miles, that the most impressive architectural landmarks of the eighteenth and nineteenth centuries are located. The main squares of the city are designed so as to afford a view of the Neva. During its entire history the architects and builders of St Petersburg did their best to make the stream of the river as beautiful as possible. In the second half of the eighteenth century the banks of "the beauty of the North" began to be clad in granite and provided with piers. The latter were often decorated with sculptures, vases and exotic statuary. The Neva was and has remained a transit navigable waterway of world significance. Passenger and trade ships can be often seen on their

The Peter Embankment. Decorative Mongol sculpture: **Shi-tsi**
The cruiser **Aurora**
The Field of Mars. Monument to the army leader Alexander Suvorov
The Neva. The Trinity (Kirovsky) Bridge

way to the Baltic Sea or from it. On festive days battleships of the Baltic Fleet, which was founded by Peter the Great, are parading moored in line along the Neva. One of the battleships, the cruiser *Aurora*, has found its permanent berth there as a memorial of the revolution. The Neva, never losing its significance as the city's main pulsating artery, has divided it into several parts. At first people crossed the river by ferryboats, then came a period of pontoon bridges, which eventually, in the second half of the nineteenth century, began to be replaced by permanent ones. Eight drawbridges span the Neva, each of them being a complex work of engineering and architecture.

The bridges look like triumphal gates over the powerful waters of the Neva, and during the hours when ships are let through them to the sea, they open their wings in a gesture of welcome.

The Summer Gardens, laid out simultaneously with the foundation of the city, are organically linked with the Neva. They are situated on an island limited by the left bank of the Neva on the north, by the Fontanka River on the east, by the Swan Canal on the west, and the Moika on the south. A remarkable feature of the garden on the Neva side is a unique forged railing with a granite base, columns, vases and gilded decorative details. It was created to the design of Yury Velten in 1771–74.
The railing on the side of the Moika was designed by Ludwig Charlemagne.
The main building in the garden is a two-storey brick palace. Its inner layout and

The Summer Gardens. The Neva railing.
The Main Gate

Sculpture: **Peace and Abundance**

decorative embellishment make the palace a notable example of Russian interiors of the early eighteenth century. The walls in the rooms are lined with cloth, the ceilings are adorned with picturesque paintings and moulded ornaments, the furnaces are faced with painted tiles, the floors are laid in the shape of geometrical patterns.
The palace was used as the private apartments of Peter the Great and Catherine I (there were seven rooms on each floor). Domenico Trezzini played the major part in the creation of the palace and the garden. The palace fronts are decorated with twenty-nine terracotta bas-reliefs to the designs of Andreas Schlüter.
The palace has retained works of art from the early eighteenth century, painted

ceilings, a very complicated instrument in a carved mount designed in Germany for measuring the wind, and a carved panel featuring *Minerva*, a work by the sculptor Nicolas Pineau, in the vestibule.

The garden, laid out in 1704, has been fashioned in a regular style. Drawing on Peter the Great's notes, the gardeners Jan Roosen and Ivan Surmin carried out initial layout work and planted first trees. The architect Jean-Baptiste Le Blond was mainly responsible for the further development of the layout. A fine decorative feature of the Summer Gardens is a large group of marble statues dating from the late seventeenth and early eighteenth centuries. The statues were bought by Russian agents on the orders of Peter the Great or executed from drawings and sketches sent from Russia. There were more than 250 sculptures in Peter's age, including authentic ancient pieces, which are now kept in the Hermitage.

The eighty-nine statues put on display in the garden nowadays reveal the depth of Peter's concept, who wanted to make his

Decorative sculpture of the 17th to the early 18th century

The Rossi Avenue

Detail of the railing on the south side of the Summer Gardens

Sculpture: **Cupid and Psyche**

The Summer Palace of Peter the Great

gardens a sort of academy. Of especial artistic value are works carved by the brilliant Venetian sculptors Pietro Baratta, Giovanni Bonazza, Giovanni Zorzone, Antonio Tarsia, and the Giuseppe brothers. Another essential feature in the concept of the gardens used to be its fountains, with water supplied by means of special machines from the river known as the Fontanka — it owes its name to the fountains, now extinct. Despite numerous losses, the Summer Gardens and the Summer Palace have retained their significance as important monuments of history, architecture and culture surviving from the age of Peter the Great.

Avenue in the Summer Gardens

The Summer Palace. The Bedroom of Peter the Great

The Study of Peter the Great

View of the Menshikov Palace from the left bank of the Neva

The Menshikov Palace, which personifies the age of the transformation of Russia and the foundation of St Petersburg, stands out in the architectural panorama of the right bank of the Neva attracting one's attention by its distinct appearance. Alexander Menshikov was the closest friend and favourite of Peter the Great, his companion in arms on the battlefield and in sea battles, his energetic assistant in state affairs and the first Governor of St Petersburg since 1703. His power and influence at the court were really great. Menshikov was, to quote the words of the poet Alexander Pushkin, a "half-ruling sovereign".

In the first quarter of the eighteenth century Menshikov's palace was the most significant and famous stately edifice mentioned by foreign ambassadors.

It was the venue for formal receptions, not only arranged by "His Highness" in honour of the monarch, but also held on behalf of Peter and Catherine for courtiers, generals and diplomats.

The grounds now occupied by the palace were used since 1704. In 1710–12 the construction of the present-day palace to the design of Marion Giovanni Fontana began. Then, until 1727, it was further decorated and extended by the architect Johann Gottfried Schädel who was employed by Menshikov.

The palace served as a permanent winter residence of the General-Field-Marshal and the Governor. From 1732 to 1965 the former Menshikov Palace was occupied by various military institutions. After the main amount of restoration work (still under way) has been completed, in 1981 the palace has begun to work as a museum. The most remarkable interior in the palace is the Walnut Drawing Room or Study, faced with wooden panels having elegant carved details. The ceiling is embellished with authentic painting representing Peter the Great in the guise of an ancient army leader. Worthy of particular note for their unique decor are the so-called " Varvara's Apartments" — the walls, stoves and ceilings there are faced with painted Delft tiles framed in moulded ornaments.

The Menshikov Palace allows its visitors to form an idea of the material decoration of a home during the age of Peter the Great and, moreover, provides an insight into its spiritual atmosphere as well.

The Menshikov Palace. The Walnut Study

"Varvara's Apartments". The Bedroom

The Winter Palace. The north front

Palace Square

The west front of the Winter Palace

The Winter Palace with its huge dimensions, rich decorative scheme and grand appearance is a personification of the might of the Russian Empire and the supreme power of its autocrat. The palace was built on the left bank of the Neva which had been earlier chosen for his modest structures by Peter the Great himself. Its project was designed by Francesco Bartolomeo Rastrelli, an architect of genius, who also supervised the initial phase of its realization. Started in 1754, during the reign of Elizabeth Petrovna, the palace was basically completed in 1762, when Catherine the Great was on the throne. The appearance of the palace has survived practically without major alterations — only decorative sculptures of Pudost stone were replaced by statues of sheet copper. An idea of Rastrelli's concept can be received in such resplendent interiors as the Jordan Staircase, the Church and the galleries of the ground floor. In the later years of the eighteenth century the state rooms and living apartments were redesigned

The Winter Palace and the Hermitage

The Winter Palace.
The Main (Jordan) Staircase

The Winter Palace. The Throne
Room of Peter the Great

by the architects Yury Velten, Jean Vallin de La Mothe and Antonio Rinaldi. The new rooms and halls were designed by Ivan Starov and Giacomo Quarenghi. In the first decades of the nineteenth century active in the Hermitage were the architects Carlo Rossi, Alexander Briullov and Auguste de Montferrand. After the fire of 1837 had erased practically all the interiors, many of them were restored, under the supervision of Vasily Stasov and Alexander Briullov, to their former appearance or designed in a new fashion. In the middle of the second half of the nineteenth century the interiors meeting the taste of the then reigning monarch

were designed by Andrei Stakenschneider, Harold Bosse and Alexander Krasovsky. The history of each, even smaller, rooms of the Winter Palace are pages in the history of court and daily life of the Imperial family. Even factual information gives an idea of the huge size of the building: it is about 200 metres long, 10 metres wide and 30 metres tall. The palace has 1057 rooms, 117 staircases, 1786 doors and 1945 windows.

The line of magnificent palaces overlooking the Neva is continued on the Palace Embankment by the monumental façades of the two Hermitage buildings. The first of them, erected by Yury Velten and Vallin

The New Hermitage. Raphael's loggia

The Winter Palace.
The Malachite Drawing
Room

de la Mothe in 1764–68 next to the Winter Palace, is known as the Small Hermitage and was intended for works of art amassed by Catherine the Great. The growth of the Empress's collection made it necessary to put up one more building, the Large Hermitage, which was designed and built by Velten in 1771–87. Extending the row of the river façades according to Quarenghi's plans, the Hermitage Theatre, linked with the Large Hermitage by the gallery over the Winter Canal, was built in 1783–89.

Few people could enjoy seeing the sculpture and rich collections of decorative and applied art kept in the Hermitage buildings and in the Winter Palace. This prompted an idea to erect a special museum building with its layout meeting a demand to arrange exhibitions of vari-ous kinds of art so that the design of display rooms would echo the age to which the exhibits belonged. The New Hermitage was constructed to the design of the German architect Leo von Klenze between 1742 and 1851. The portico of the New Hermitage was embellished with the famous granite Atlantes hewn by St Petersburg stone-carvers from models by Alexander Terebenev.

Walking along the suites of state rooms in the Winter Palace and the Hermitages, you can enjoy really superb examples of interior decoration ranking with the world's best achievements. Worthy of special mention are the Throne Room of Peter the Great designed by Montferrand; the 1812 War Gallery by Rossi; the St George Hall (or Great Throne Room) by Quarenghi; the Great Anteroom and the Armorial Hall by Quarenghi and Stasov; the Malachite Drawing Room, the Rotunda and the Alexander Room by Briullov, the Golden Drawing Room and the Pavilion Hall by Stakenschneider and Raphael's Loggias by Quarenghi. The sumptuous interiors, which attract our attention themselves, house priceless

The Winter Palace. The St George Hall

The Winter Palace. The Golden Drawing Room

The Winter Palace. The Boudoir

*Leonardo da Vinci. **The Litta Madonna**. Ca. 1490–91*

creations of human genius from all ages and nations. Making a tour of the rooms, halls and galleries, you plunge into different ages and familiarize yourselves with the cultures of various peoples inhabiting our planet. Each exhibit here, down to the smallest item, is priceless. But in the same way as even in an array of gems or diamonds some pieces of exceptional value can be singled out, so the collection of the Hermitage boasts a number of really unique works known

*Rembrandt. **Danaë**. 1636*

*El Greco. **The Apostles Peter and Paul**. Between 1587 and 1592*

all over the world. The museum collections contain first-rate artifacts of primitive culture, superb works of art dating from Classical Antiquity, masterpieces of painting by Leonardo da Vinci, Giorgione, Titian, Rembrandt, El Greco, Paul Rubens, Anthony van Dyck and Jacob Jordaens. French art of the eighteenth to the twentieth century is represented by such renowned names as Nicolas Poussin, Antoine Watteau, Jean-Baptiste Chardin, Pierre-Auguste Renoir, Paul Cézanne, Vincent van Gogh, Paul Gauguin, Pablo Picasso and Henri Matisse. The list can be endlessly extended to include other great French, German, Italian, Spanish and English painters, sculptors, designers whose art was marked by outstanding artistic achievements and pioneering discoveries which determined the styles

Rembrandt. **The Return of the Prodigal Son**. *Late 1660s*

Pieter Paul Rubens. **The Union of Earth and Water.** *Between 1612 and 1615*

Auguste Rodin. **Eternal Spring. 1897**

The Gonzaga cameo. 3rd century B.C.

Comb from the Solokha barrow. 4th century B.C.

Paul Gauguin. **Woman Holding a Fruit**. *1893*

Pablo Picasso. **Woman with a Fan (After a Ball)**. *1908*

*Henri Matisse. **The Red Room**. 1908*

of the ages. The pride of the Hermitage Museum are rare works by European sculptors such as Michelangelo, Bernini, Canova, Thorwaldsen and Rodin as well as the largest numismatic collection in Russia. The Department of Russian Culture is also notable for its wealth and variety. It is hardly possible to imagine a kind of art that is not represented in the Hermitage. The Hermitage complex is a veritable spiritual universe created in the course of the times by means of the godly gifts named creativity and art.

The Hermitage Theatre linked with the Large (Old) Hermitage by the gallery spanning the Winter Canal, forms, together with the stone Hermitage Bridge at the confluence of the canal and the Neva, one of the most poetic architectural sights of St Petersburg.

No less impressive is the portico of the New Hermitage with its granite figures of Atlantes supporting a massive balcony. The Hermitage Theatre was built by Giacomo Quarenghi on the site of Peter the Great's Winter Palace in the austere Classical style on the orders of Catherine the Great for performances staged at the court since the eighteenth century on various festive occasions. This festive

The Hermitage Theatre

*The New Hermitage.
Portico with Atlantes*

The Winter Canal

*Perspective view
of the Winter Canal*

designation was stressed by the imposing decor of the auditorium embellished with painting and sculpture.

The architect has preserved some Peter's interiors within the Hermitage Theatre. The Winter Canal connecting the Neva with the Moika was dug out by 1719. Originally it was named the Winter Palace Canal — after the Peter the Great's palace then standing on its left bank. Three bridges were built over the canal to enhance the effect of a perspective view. You will hardly find many equally delightful sights in the whole city. The Winter Canal is well known almost all over the world, at least in all the countries where Tchaikovsky's opera *The Queen of Spades* was staged.

Palace Square dominates the historical centre of St Petersburg. Its spatial solution was created by Carlo Rossi in 1819–29. The square is remarkable for its harmonious blend of the monumental General Staff building, the elegant Imperial Palace, the monolithic granite column with the Angel on the top, which is set in its centre to the design of Auguste de Montferrand, and the austere building of the Guards Headquarters designed by Alexander Briullov. Palace Square is a sort of architectural centerpiece crowning the northern capital of Russia.

Panoramic view of Palace Square from the Arch of the General Staff building

The Arch of the General Staff building. The Chariot of Glory (Victory)

Panoramic view of Palace Square. The Alexander Column

The Admiralty. The Triumphal Gate (detail)

The Main Admiralty building. Tower with the Triumphal Gate

One of the city's major architectural landmarks, second only to the Peter and Paul Fortress, is the Admiralty founded in 1704 as a fortress and shipyard. A century later the original layout of the shipyard was further developed by the architect Andreyan Zakharov whose plans and drawings were used in 1806–19 to erect the building with its façade stretching for over 400 metres and its side fronts for more than 170 metres. The central section is accentuated by the three-tiered tower with a 72-metre-tall spire and by the base bearing a gateway designed similarly to the Arche de Triomphe in Paris.

The statues and high reliefs feature sea motifs and subjects from the history of the Russian Navy. The monumental

The Admiralty

The south front of the Admiralty

groups of nymphs are executed of Pudost stone and cast of alabaster from models by Ivan Terebenev and Feodosy Shchedrin. All the structures of the Admiralty with their majestic architectural design and sculptural decoration glorify the heroism of Russian sailors and of Peter the Great as the creator of St Petersburg, the capital of the Russian Navy and the trade fleet.

The Admiralty. Decorative sculpture

The Lt Schmidt Embankment. Monument to Admiral Ivan Krusenstern

The Palace Embankment. Monument: **The Tsar-Shipwright**

51

A notable feature in the panorama of the right bank of the Neva is the austere, monumental building of the Academy of Arts. Its central part is given prominence by a portico surmounted with a low dome. The extensive building with an overall height of 35.5 metres was put up according to designs by the architects Alexander Kokorinov and Jean-Baptiste Vallin de la Mothe in 1764–89 and its inauguration ceremony was held in the presence of Catherine the Great.

The Academy of Arts, set up by Empress Elizabeth Petrovna in 1757, is one of the largest buildings in the city. It was to house a higher educational establishment

The University Embankment. Pier with sphinxes

*View of the Academy of Arts from
the Lt Schmidt Bridge*

The Conference Hall of the Academy of Arts

View of the University Embankment

intended for training Russian artists, sculptors and architects.

All major academic events took place in the large Conference Hall, the dome of which is painted with a festivity on Olympus celebrating the establishment of the fine arts in Russia.

Almost all great Russian artists were students of the Academy of Arts, and it still keeps the best creative traditions of the past developing them.

The granite pier that adorns the Neva embankment in front of the Academy of Arts is embellished with bronze lamps and two statues of ancient Egyptian sphinxes brought from Egypt in a ship hold under grain in 1732.

The pier with sphinxes, together with the entire complex of the Academy of Arts, has become a well-known symbol of St Petersburg as a city of the arts. Many artists depicted this splendid architectural view. Eminent Russian poets such as Alexander Blok and Valery Briusov devoted poetic lines to the sphinxes.

The Admiralty Embankment. The Palace Pier

The Kunstkammer. View from the left bank of the Neva

The Mikhailovsky Castle (the Russian Museum). The south front

One of Rossi's famous masterpieces is the complex of the Mikhailovsky Palace built for Grand Duke Mikhail Pavlovich, brother of Emperor Nicholas I, in 1819–25. The architectural decor of its interiors which is associated with the victory of Russia in the 1812 War against Napoleon Bonaparte, is strikingly harmonious.

In 1888, on the order of Emperor Alexander III, the building of the palace suitable for a display of paintings, began to be converted into a museum of Russian art. Now the State Russian Museum contains the world's largest collection of works by Russian painters, sculptors, graphic artists, designers and craftsmen from the tenth century to the present day.

Mikhailovskaya Square. Monument to the poet Alexander Pushkin. 1957. Sculptor Mikhail Anikushin

Two original interiors designed by Rossi have survived — the Main Vestibule and the White-Columned Hall. The vast vestibule occupies the entire central part of the building, the ceiling of which is painted in grisaille in imitation of sculptural and architectural decor.

The White-Columned Hall, faced with artificial marble from top to bottom, is notable for the ensemble of its painted decoration, parquet floor and furnishings which has been retained intact. This hall is one of the most perfect interiors in the architecture of Russian Classicism. It helps us imagine the St Petersburg of Pushkin's era — that formal setting in which members of "high society" and the characters described in *Eugene Onegin*, the poet's famous novel in verse, used to spend their time.

The main vestibule of the Russian Museum

The Exhibition Hall. Architect Vasily Svinyin

The White-Columned Hall

Icon: **The Archangel Gabriel (The Angel with the Golden Hair).** *11th century*

*Icon: **The Miracle of St George**. 16th century*

victims of intestine strife, were canonized, and the crosses in their hands suggest their holiness.

Another masterpiece owned by the museum is the fifteenth-century icon devoted to the life and deeds of St George. Visitors to the rooms of ancient Russian art can also see works by the great icon-painters Andrei Rublev, Dionysius and Simon Ushakov, artists of world stature.

Adapted in the 1880s for the needs of the museum, the interiors of the Mikhailovsky Palace combine

*Icon: **SS Boris and Gleb**. 15th century*

The Russian Museum possesses one of the largest collections of ancient Russian fine arts. Chronologically its exhibition covers a period from the ninth century throughout the seventeenth. The exhibits include examples of wall paintings and mosaics from ancient Russian churches of the Kiev State. The Department of Ancient Russian Art consists largely of icons, a highly original and expressive kind of painting. The gem of the collection is one of the earliest works in the Russian Museum — the icon *The Archangel Gabriel (Angel with the Golden Hair)*. Few works in world art can rival this masterpiece, permeated with a lyrical quality, in the power of emotional impact. The icon *Boris and Gleb* featuring the portrait-like images of the two princes, sons of Grand Prince Vladimir, is pervaded with the spirit of austere majesty. Every detail of the representation, from the princes' hats and garments to their swords, is historically authentic. Princes Boris and Gleb,

The Russian Museum. Suite of rooms

all distinguished by their powerful brushwork and brilliance of manner, while some of them attest him as a virtuoso of painting.

The most celebrated work by Briullov, which not only made the artist famous in Russia but won him European renown, is *The Last Day of Pompeii*.

Six years passed from the first concept,

Karl Briullov. **The Last Day of Pompeii.** *1833*

the majestic state decor with a possibility to arrange the displays chronologically. The suite design of the interiors, perfectly suitable for this purpose, affords an impressive perspective view of the exhibition rooms.

The Russian Museum owns the most significant part of the creative legacy of Karl Briullov, an outstanding painter active in the first half of the nineteenth century. The Briullov Room presents all the variety of the painter's work: from genre scenes and formal portraits painted in the manner of elaborate subject paintings to rather small intimate self-portraits and likenesses of his contemporaries. Briullov's canvases are which emerged in 1827, to the completion of the huge canvas featuring the eruption of Mount Vesuvius in the year 79 that buried under volcanic ash the ancient Roman town of Pompeii. Briullov painted the subject like a historian thoroughly studying the contemporary evidence of the tragic event. Moreover, Briullov presented the event — so remote from him — as if he witnessed the drama. The pivot of his work is the power of human spirit revealed during a sudden natural calamity. It is to this quality that the scene, largely a theatrical display with showy painterly effects, owes its tragic intensity. Ivan Aivazovsky, a great marine painter, is world-famous for his monumental

Ilya Repin. **The Zaporozhye Cossacks Writing a Mocking Letter to the Turkish Sultan.** *1878–91*

Ivan Aivazovsky. **The Ninth Wave.** *1850*

seascapes. An inspired poet of the sea, Aivazovsky was incomparable in his ability to capture the soul of the "free elements" during a storm and in a still weather, in moonlight and under the glistening stars, in the rays of the setting sun and in daytime. He also took up battle painting devoting a number of his works to the campaigns of the Russian Navy.

The museum's fine selection of works by Ilya Repin provides an opportunity to trace the career of this powerful and versatile talent at different periods and

Kuzma Petrov-Vodkin. **The Death of a Commissar.** *1927*

in various facets of his art — as a great portraitist, a master of socially oriented genre scenes or as a painter of historical subjects. His most popular canvas in this series is the *Zaporozhye Cossacks Writing a Mocking Letter to the Turkish Sultan*.

A brilliant and highly individual phenomenon in Russian art of the first three decades of the twentieth century was the work of Kuzma Petrov-Vodkin, an artist who created a distinctive compositional and colouristic system of his own.

An illustrious example is his painting *The Death of a Commissar* marked with his characteristic spherical composition and unusual colour range.

The art of the early twentieth century

Nathan Altman. *Portrait of Anna Akhmatova. 1914*

Wassily Kandinsky. *Composition No 224. 1920*

Kasimir Malevich. *Peasants. 1928–32*

Pavel Filonov. **The Formula of Spring.** *1927–29*

is represented in the Russian Museum by works of world significance. *The Portrait of Anna Akhmatova*, painted by Nathan Altman in 1914, is notable for its use of devices introduced by Cubism. Kasimir Malevich, the founder of an innovative trend known as Suprematism, earned wide acclaim with his canvas *Black Square* of 1913 and his spatial compositions called "architectons". Wassily Kandinsky, who painted his first abstract pictures as early as 1910, followed by a series of non-representational "improvisations" and "compositions", is considered to be the initiator of Abstract Art.

Among the "stellar" ideas characteristic of the avant-garde in the first quarter of the twentieth century the leading role belongs to Pavel Filonov, who created a movement known as Analytical Art. Anticipating the arrival of the cosmic era, Filonov sought to penetrate into the metaphysics of the Universe and to realize his insights in vibrant painting.

St Isaaç's Square

The ensemble of St Isaac's Square is a link in the grandiose architectural and artistic complex of the squares on the left bank of the Neva. The square lies in the area where construction began with the foundation of St Petersburg. It was occupied by the structures of the Sea Settlement connected with the Admiralty, which was then both fortress and wharf. The present-day names of the streets crossing the square — Large and Small Morskaya Streets — remind us of this historical fact.

The square is lined with monumental buildings serving as a sort of its architectural frame which took shape between the eighteenth and early twentieth centuries. The chronology of these buildings, reflected in their stylistic features, confirms that the architecture of St Isaac's Square has been created in the course of about three centuries. The compositional and spiritual focus of the square is St Isaac's Cathedral. The cathedral and square are named in honour of St Isaac of Dalmatia whose feast day is on 30 May, the date when the birthday of Peter the Great is celebrated. Therefore, St Isaac's Square was regarded in the system of squares personifying the capital of the Empire as a majestic approach to the main church of the state. This fact determined the scale and decor of the two symmetrical buildings of ministries put up to designs by the architect Nikolai Yefimov in 1844–53.

In 1859 an equestrian monument to Emperor Nicholas I was unveiled in the centre of the square. Auguste de Montferrand was in charge of its architectural concept; the emperor's figure was sculpted by Piotr Klodt; the allegorical figures of Faith, Wisdom, Power and Justice, with the features reminiscent of those of the emperor's wife and daughters, were created by Robert Zaleman; the four bas-reliefs were produced by Nikolai Ramazanov and Zaleman.

In 1911–12 two new buildings were fitted into the composition of the square — the German Embassy by Peter Behrens and the Astoria Hotel by Fiodor Lidval. The appearance of the first edifice is suggestive of a tendency towards pomp; while Astoria is designed in the fashion of St Petersburg Art Nouveau. Nevertheless, both later buildings matched the ensemble and harmoniously completed the composition of St Isaac's Square.

The huge St Isaac's Cathedral, 101.5 metres high, faced with marble and crowned with a giant dome and smaller cupolas over belfries, dominates the surrounding area. The four porticoes are emphasized with 72 monolithic granite columns weighing from 64 to 114 tons. Started in 1818, the cathedral was built for forty years to plans by Auguste de Montferrand. St Isaac's is decorated with 350 reliefs and statues. The entire sculptural decoration of the cathedral

was executed from models by Ivan Vitali, Stepan Pimenov, Alexander Loganovsky, Piotr Klodt and Philippe Lemaire. The wealth of sculptural decoration united by Biblical subjects perfectly blends with the overall architectural scheme of the cathedral. St Isaac's is one of the highest achievements in the synthesis of arts during that period. The interior of the cathedral is marked by an unusual wealth of decor and the abundance of rare and valuable materials used in it. Coloured stones and different

North portico of St Isaac's. High relief:
The Ascension of Christ

Angels with lamps

St Isaac's Square. Monument to Nicholas I

The drum of the main dome

The nave and the main iconostasis of St Isaac's

kinds of marble are skilfully used there in a great variety of patterns. The iconostasis is adorned with white Italian marble, gilded bronze and decorative sculptures featuring angels and prophets. The impression of unusual richness and luxury is enhanced by the polychrome painted panels and canvases.

The interior is embellished with 150 pictures and ceiling paintings, which are veritable masterpieces of Russian monumental art of the mid-nineteenth century.

View of the Mariinsky Palace

The south side of St Isaac's Square is taken up by the Mariinsky Palace. It is connected with the square by the Blue Bridge spanning the Moika. This is the widest bridge in the city (97.3 metres wide and 32.5 metres long). The first wooden bridge was built here in 1730 and in 1818 it was replaced with a cast-iron one built to the design of William Geste. The name of the palace erected by Andrei Stakenschneider in 1839–44 suggests that its first owner was Grand Duchess Maria Nikolayevna, daughter of Nicholas I. In the eighteenth century the site was occupied by the palace of Count Ivan Chernyshov, a courtier of Catherine the Great, and by three other structures. They were demolished to put up an extensive building decorated with columns and pilasters. The main entrance is emphasized with an arcade and vases and the centre

The Mariinsky Palace. The Church

The main façade of the Mariinsky Palace

The Mariinsky Palace. The Rotunda

of the building is crowned with an attic. The palace was designed so as to meet the demands of everyday and festive life of the Grand Duchess. The interiors were adorned with especial luxury and elegance, with the use of expensive materials, precious kinds of wood and marble. Particularly remarkable for their stately appearance were the Reception Room, the Rotunda, the Large (Square) Hall, the Concert (Dance) Hall and the Palace Church.

The Mariinsky Palace is one of the most perfect works of Andrei Stakenschneider and a typical architec-tural monument of the mid-nineteenth century.

The Kazan Cathedral. The main façade

The House of Books (the former Singer Company building)

Amidst the domes "soaring" above the city there can be clearly seen the cross of the Kazan Cathedral glistening at the height of nearly 64 metres. The cathedral was named in honour of the icon of the Mother of God miraculously found during the storm of Kazan by the troops of Ivan the Terrible. The icon became one of national symbols and in 1612–13, during the Time of Troubles, it was kept in the travelling church of the militia, led by Prince Dmitry Pozharsky, which liberated Moscow from the Polish troops. In 1710, to establish the prestige of St Petersburg, an icon similar to the Kazan image in subject and composition was brought to St Petersburg from Moscow. Emperor Paul I, who had visited Rome before ascending the throne, ordered that a stone cathedral modelled on St Peter's be built in Nevsky Prospekt, the main thorough-fare of St Petersburg. The project designed by Andrei Voronikhin with the assistance of Count Alexander Stroganov, President of the Academy of Arts, was approved

Monument to Field-Marshal Barclay de Tolly

by the emperor and in August 1801 the ceremony of its foundation was held. Ten years later, on 27 September 1811, the cathedral was consecrated in a festive atmosphere.

Voronikhin showed himself an architect of genius — although he received the Imperial order to "follow the model", he succeeded in creating a unique example of the Russian church. The composition of the cathedral is remarkable for the powerful sweep of its arc of 24 columns set in four rows, all carved of Pudost stone. The central part of the cathedral is supported by the six-columned portico surmounted with a triangular pediment bearing the gilded symbol of the Divine Eye. The portico has a bronze door, a copy of the "Gate of Paradise" in the Baptistery of Florence executed in 1425–52 by the sculptor Lorenzo Ghiberti and the four bronze statues — *St John the Baptist*

by Ivan Martos, *St Andrew the First Called* by Ivan Prokofyev, and *St Vladimir Equal of the Apostles and St Alexander Nevsky* by Stepan Pimenov. These works were aimed to suggest in an allegorical form that the Orthodox Church was directly linked with early Christianity. The cathedral is the burial place of Field Marshal Mikhail Kutuzov. The crypt with the grave of the army leader, a hero of the 1812 War against Napoleon Bonaparte, the captured standards and other objects associated with the Russian Army made the Kazan Cathedral significant as a major monument of military glory. In front of the cathedral, at either end of the colonnade, stand the statues of Field-Marshal Mikhail Kutuzov and Mikhail Barclay de Tolly (1837, sculptor Boris Orlovsky).

The Last Judgement. *Detail of a 18th-century icon. The Kazan Cathedral*

The Kazan Cathedral. The nave

Nevsky Prospekt is the most important and well-known street in the historical centre of St Petersburg loved by the inhabitants of the city and attracting its numerous tourists.

In 1710 two roads, from the Admiralty and from the St Alexander Nevsky Lavra, were laid down. In 1760 they merged into a single arterial thoroughfare. In 1738 it was named Nevskaya Perspective and in 1783 renamed Nevsky Prospekt.

The overall length of Nevsky Prospekt is 4.5 kilometres, its width varies from 25 to 60 metres. The ensemble of the prospekt includes many outstanding architectural landmarks of the eighteenth to twentieth century.

Nevsky Prospekt
The Yeliseyev Food Shop
The Alexandrine Theatre
Monument to Catherine the Great

A notable feature of Nevsky Prospekt is the Alexandrine Theatre (named after Pushkin), one of the most perfect creations by Carlo Rossi erected in 1828–32. In 1783 a monument to Catherine the Great, the work of Mikhail Mikeshin, Alexander Opekushin and Matvei Chizhov, was set up in front of the theatre. Around the towering figure of the empress were placed the major figures of her reign.

The Fontanka Embankment. The Beloselsky-Belozersky Palace

View from a window of the Drawing Room of the Beloselsky-Belozersky Palace

View from a window of the Drawing Room of the Beloselsky-Belozersky Palace

Nevsky Prospekt crosses the Fontanka, one of the largest waterways in St Petersburg (it is about 7 kilometres long and up to 70 metres wide). Until the middle of the eighteenth century the river served as a boundary of the city. In 1780–89 its banks were faced with granite, provided with steps and ramps for the landing of cargo boats. There are 15 bridges across the Fontanka, some of which were built in the second half of the eighteenth century. The most celebrated of them is perhaps the Anichkov Bridge. It is 54.6 metres long and 38 metres wide. The bridge owes its name to a certain officer, Anichkov, who built it in wood during the reign of Peter the Great. The present-day structure was designed in 1841 by the engineer Andrei Gotman. Its cast-iron handrails with relief representations of mermaids, tridents and ornaments are ascribed to the architect Alexander Briullov. Between 1833 and the 1850s the granite pillars of the bridge were decorated with four sculptural groups, *Taming a Horse*, cast of bronze to designs by Piotr Klodt. The fronts of the Beloselsky-Belozersky Palace overlook both the Fontanka and Nevsky Prospekt. Designed by Andrei Stakenschneider and decorated by the sculptor David Iensen (1846–48), the palace is a stylized Baroque edifice in the spirit of Rastrelli's works. From 1884 the palace became the residence of Grand Duke Sergei Alexandrovich, the fourth son of Emperor Alexander II.

The Anichkov Bridge. Sculptural group:
Taming the Horse. *1846–50. Sculptor Piotr Klodt*

The Anichkov Bridge

The Marble Palace. Statue of Alexander III. 1906. Sculptor Paolo Trubetskoi

The Marble Palace. The south front

The Marble Palace. Bas-reliefs

The Marble Palace, an outstanding example of St Petersburg architecture, was created for Prince Grigory Orlov, a favourite of Catherine the Great, to designs by Antonio Rinaldi in 1768—85. 32 kinds of northern and Italian marbles were used for the sheathing of its fronts and for its interior decoration. The palace was richly embellished with statuary by Mikhail Kozlov and Fedot Shubin. The Marble Palace is Rinaldi's highest accomplishment and a masterpiece of St Petersburg architecture. One of the most notable features of the palace is the harmony of its natural coloured stones, the Neva waters and the northern sky. Nowadays the palace houses a branch of the Russian Museum.

The Marble Palace

The Mikhailovsky Castle. The south front. Monument to Peter the Great

The Mikhailovsky (Engineers') Castle, the most mysterious and Romantic building in St Petersburg and in the entire Russian architecture of the late eighteenth century, has never failed to attract attention of not only researchers in architecture, but of historians, writers and poets too. Built by the orders of Paul I as a fortress or castle, it became a trap for the emperor who was killed in this building during the night of 12 March 1801.

The mystically inclined Emperor trusted the dream of a soldier who had guarded the wooden palace of Elizabeth Petrovna where Paul had been born. The soldier told that the Archangel Michael appeared to him in a dream and commanded that a palace be built on the emperor's birthplace for his long life there. Paul I ordered to demolish the Elizabethan structure and to put up a new palace on the site. The construction began to the design of Vasily Bazhenov, but was continued according to drawings by Vincenzo Brenna in 1797–1800. The south front has completely retained Bazhenov's design, while the other parts were partly altered; the interior decor was executed from Brenna's sketches. Paul I ordered to place in front of the castle the equestrian statue of Peter the Great, a 1747 work by Carlo Bartolomeo Rastrelli bearing the inscrip-

The Mikhailovsky Palace. The Church of the Archangel Michael. Iconostasis

The Mikhailovsky Castle. The Moika Embankment

tion: "To the Great-Grandfather from the Great-Grandson." On either side of the northern front are set up huge bronze sculptures of *Hercules* and *Flora*, copies from famous Greek originals.

The castle was built as an impregnable citadel — it was protected by the Fontanka on the east, the Moika on the north, and canals were dug on the other sides. In spite of all the fortified contrivances, drawbridges and reinforced guard, the conspirators penetrated to Paul's bedroom and smothered him there as he refused to abdicate.

The Rossi Pavilion

Hercules of Farnese.
Late 18th-century copy. Bronze

Many panoramic sights of St Petersburg afford picturesque views of the nine-domed Cathedral of the Resurrection which is 81 metres high. It was put up on the bank of the Griboyedov Canal — on the site where the 63-year-old Emperor Alexander II was mortally wounded by the terrorist Ignaty Grinevitsky who exploded a hand-made bomb. The emperor died on the same day in the Winter Palace. To commemorate the 26-year reign of the Tsar, who entered the history of Russia as the "Liberator" of peasants from serfdom, and to redeem the sin of regicide, this unique cathedral commonly known as "Our Saviour-on-the Spilt-Blood" was built for funds raised by people's donations. The artistic concept of the cathedral goes back to examples of the Moscow and Yaroslavl architecture and particularly to the famous Moscow Cathedral of St Basil the Blessed. Legend has it that the general idea of its unusual design came in a dream to the senior priest of the Trinity-St Sergius Monastery Archimandrite Ignaty (Malyshev). Possessing professional artistic skills, he worked on the project together with the architect Alfred Parland.
The ceremony of the foundation of the cathedral was held on 14 September 1883. The cathedral was consecrated on 19 August 1907 in the presence of Emperor Nicholas II and the entire most august family.
The twenty-four years of construction work resulted in the creation of a masterpiece of architecture, not only in terms of St Petersburg but of Russia as a whole, linking, as it were, the northern capital with the ancient roots of Russian creativity.
The Cathedral of the Resurrection is literally a precious piece of work.

The Cathedral of the Resurrection.
The central tent-shaped tower, domes
and the cupola of the bell-tower

The interior of the cathedral covered all over with mosaic representations on subjects from the Old and New Testaments may be compared to a shrine. The precious four-columned jasper canopy emphasized the spot on the road where the Tsar's blood was spilt.
The mosaics were produced at the Frolov workshop in St Petersburg from sketches by Mikhail Nesterov, Andrei Riabushkin and other eminent artists. The history of art knows but a few examples of such a large-scale mosaic project — 6,000 square metres in the interiors and 1,050 square metres of the exterior walls are decorated with mosaics.

→

*The west façade. Mosaic: **The Crucifixion**. From a sketch by Alfred Parland*

*The Cathedral of the Resurrection.
Mosaic in the apse: **The Eucharist***

The Griboyedov Canal. The Bank Bridge

The Fontanka River. The Egyptian Bridge

The Griboyedov Canal which starts from the Moika near the Field of Mars, crosses the old regions of the city and empties into the Fontanka. It came into being when the Kriusha River was linked with the Moika. Later, in the eighteenth and nineteenth centuries, the hydrotechnical system of the canal was improved and its embankments acquired an imposing architectural look. Of the twenty bridges spanning the canal two are particularly famous: the Bank Bridge and the Lion Bridge. The first of them was built in front of the State Bank and decorated with fabulous winged creatures. The Lion Bridge is adorned with four realistically rendered iron lions, hence its name. The Egyptian Bridge, a chain bridge across the Fontanka designed by the engineers Georg Tretter and V. Kristianevich, owes its name to the four cast-iron sphinxes, a free imita-

tion of ancient Egyptian art. In 1905
the bridge collapsed when a squadron of
the Horse Guards Regiment marched over
it. Only in 1955 a permanent up-to-date
bridge has been built in this place, but
nothing has remained of the former one
except for the sphinxes.

St Petersburg rivers and canals are remarkable as fascinating ensembles which are set
with gems of architecture suddenly emerg-
ing among usual buildings.

A noteworthy example is the monumental
arch of the complex of naval timber
warehouses on the Moika named "New
Holland". The impressive arch was
designed Savva Chevakinsky and Vallin
de la Mothe in the 1770s–1780s.

"New Holland". The Triumphal Arch

The Griboyedov Canal. The Lion Bridge

The St Nicholas Cathedral

The Cathedral of St Nicholas and the Epiphany is regarded as a symbol of St Petersburg's blessing as a city of naval glory. Hence its common name — the Naval Cathedral — which goes back to the era of Peter the Great when the Maritime Yard was located on the site, with a wooden church as its spiritual centre. The cathedral, consisting of two churches, was designed by the architect Savva Chevakinsky. In June 1753

a ceremony of its foundation was held and nine years later the construction was completed. Creating the cathedral, Chevakinsky revealed an exclusive feeling for scale and proportion combined with a skilful use of decorative means. The building is marked by a luxurious, festive appearance characteristic of the reign of Elizabeth Petrovna. The Corinthian columns emphasize the corners of the volumes and enhance the imposing look of the building. An overall impression of lightness is further enhanced by the semicircular window apertures of the Lower and Upper Churches and of the dome towers. The lavish architectural decor and the elaborate patterns of the balcony railings are perfectly blended with the glistening of the five gilded domes and small cupolas crowned with crosses.

The theme of Russian sailors' laudatory hymn to the Lord and saint patrons is powerfully expressed in the three-dimensional composition and decoration of the Lower and Upper Churches of the cathedral. The Upper Church, consecrated on 20 July 1762 to the Epiphany, is marked by a refinement of its design. Divided by pylons soaring upwards into seven chapels, it is filled with light that multiplies a play of the brilliant gilded ornaments.

The two-tiered iconostasis, executed by the master carver Ignaty Kanayev, is remarkable both for its magnificent composition and elaborate decorative details. The icons adorning the iconostasis were painted by the well-known icon-painters, the brothers Mina and Fiodor Kolokolnikov. The cathedral's icons, which are both objects of worship and great artistic value, are worthy of particular note. The main of them is the icon showing St Nicholas, the archbishop of Myra in Asia Minor in the first half of the fourth century, a patron of Russia and of sailors.

The cathedral became the centre of prayers for the sailors who perished during the Russo-Japanese War of 1904–05. This event is recorded on two marble slabs

Interior of the Upper Church in the St Nicholas Cathedral

The Kriukov Canal. The bell-tower of the St Nicholas Cathedral

*The St Nicholas
Cathedral. Icon:*
**St Nicholas
the Miracle Worker**

*The St Nicholas
Cathedral. Icon:*
**The Three-Armed
Mother of God**

placed in the interior of the cathedral.
In 1989 this tradition was continued by
the mounting of a tablet commemorating
dead submariners.

The detached bell-tower, which forms
a single spatial composition with the
cathedral, was also designed by Savva
Chevakinsky and built in 1753–62.
A spectacular view of the bell-tower
against the waters of the Kriukov Canal
took shape later, in 1782–87, when the
man-made canal dug out during the reign
of Peter the Great, in 1719, was linked
with the Fontanka.

The Cathedral of the Holy Trinity in the Alexander Nevsky Lavra

The Alexander Nevsky Lavra (or the St Alexander Nevsky Monastery of the Holy Trinity) is the largest eighteenth-century architectural complex in St Petersburg. The monastery was founded on the orders of Peter the Great in 1710 and dedicated to the memory of Prince Alexander Nevsky who won a victory over the Swedish troops in 1240. The Alexander Nevsky Lavra was designed as a spiritual centre on the new Russian capital. Adjoining the Alexander Nevsky Lavra are the Lazarevskoye, Nikolskoye and Tikhvinskoye cemeteries, the latter being a necropolis of prominent men of arts of the nineteenth and twentieth centuries.

Tomb of Fiodor Dostoyevsky. 1883.
Sculptor N. Lavretsky, architect H. Vasilyev

Tomb of Piotr Tchaikovsky. 1897. Sculptor F. Kamensky

Religious procession. Patriarch Alexis II

The Alexander Nevsky Lavra. Interior of the Cathedral of the Holy Trinity

The Alexander Nevsky Lavra

The Cathedral of the Holy Trinity, the focal part of the monastery, is marked by the features of Classicism. Its general design, the treatment of its front and the decor of its interiors show a great talent of the architect Ivan Starov. The entrance to the cathedral is accentuated by the six-columned portico of the Roman Doric order, the interior is divided into a nave and two aisles. The perspective of the nave is emphasized by Corinthian columns with gilded capitals. The expressive figures of saints decorating the cathedral are by the sculptor Fedot Shubin. The iconostasis is adorned with Italian and Russian marbles; the Holy Gate is made of ormolu.

The Mariinsky Theatre

The auditorium of the Mariinsky Theatre

Anyone who arrives in St Petersburg even for a short time, takes efforts to see a performance at the Mariinsky (formerly Kirov) Opera and Ballet Theatre. The large building of the theatre faces a small Theatre Square named after it and the Conservatory on the opposite side. It was here, in the Stone (Bolshoi) Theatre, built in 1783, that opera, ballet and drama companies of St Petersburg staged their performances. In 1855 the opera and ballet companies were transferred to the theatre-circus erected on the site of the present-day edifice by Albert Cavos in 1847. In 1859–60 the building began to be called the Mariinsky Theatre in honour of the wife of Alexander II. In 1883–96 Victor Schröter gave to the theatre a grand appearance befitting its Imperial status.

*Scene from the ballet **Swan Lake by** Piotr Tchaikovsky*

*Scene from the opera **Boris Godunov** by Modest Mussorgsky*

The Moika Embankment. The Yusupov Palace

The Yusupov Palace on the Moika is one of those rare works of architecture whose history is closely associated with the names of the aristocracy, eminent architects and artists of the nineteenth and early twentieth century. Beyond the austere façade and six-columned Tuscan portico are richly decorated interiors. In the 1760s, on the site of the present-day building stood the mansion of General-Field-Marshal, Count Piotr Shuvalov, brother of Empress Elizabeth's favourite. In 1830 the palace on the Moika was purchased by Prince Nikolai Yusupov, a man of fabulous riches (his title, fortune and palace were inherited by the grandson's son-in-law, Count Felix Sumarokov-Elston, known as Prince Felix Yusupov.) In 1830–38 the Yusupovs commissioned the architect Andrei Mikhailov the Junior to refashion the building and he drastically altered its design. In 1858–59 the architect Hyppolito Monighetti introduced new

The Yusupov Palace. The Hall Roman

The Yusupov Palace. The Theatre

Prince Felix Yusupov and Grigory Rasputin. Display: **The Last Talk**
(wax effigies and imitation the interior)

alterations: he created the Main Staircase, redesigned the interior of the palatial theatre and renewed the decor in a number of drawing rooms stylizing them in the spirit of Oriental art. In 1860 Academician Ernest Liphart adorned the ceiling with an expressive painted decoration, made insets for box barriers and produced a curtain for the theatre.

The Yusupov Palace was the scene of a memorable tragic event in Russian history. It was in this building that during the night of 17 December 1916 the last owner of the palace, Prince Felix Yusupov, Grand Duke Dmitry Pavlovich, Vladimir Purishkevich, a deputy of the State Duma, and two other conspirators murdered Grigory Rasputin, a favourite of the royal family, in order to save the Russian throne from his influence.

The Smolny Cathedral

The Smolny Cathedral. View from the Peter the Great (Okhta) Bridge

A remarkable feature of the St Petersburg skyline is the Resurrection Cathedral of the Smolny Convent soaring high upwards on the left bank of the Neva.

The site now occupied by the convent has been inhabited before the foundation of St Petersburg — there was a settlement of the principality of Novgorod in this area in the fifteenth century, and in the seventeenth the Swedes had their fortifications and settlement in the area. Peter the Great used the territory to build a tar yard ("tar" means *smola* in Russian), hence the name of the convent. A palace put up for Catherine stood nearby (it existed from 1720 to 1760).

Elizabeth Petrovna ordered that a cathedral and a building of the Novodevichy Convent of the Resurrection be built on this site. The project designed by Bartolomeo Francesco Rastrelli, though not completely realized, was marked by a great inspiration and exquisite elaboration of the silhouette. The history of the construction was as follows: in 1748–64 the building of the cathedral was erected and its fronts were decorated; in 1832–35 the interiors were embellished in the Classical style from drawings by Vasily Stasov. The cathedral was consecrated as a place of worship for all female educational establishments of the city.

The churches of St Petersburg are worthy of special note for their historical and artistic significance. The skyline of the right bank of the Neva is punctuated by the cathedral of St Prince Vladimir, remarkable for its harmonious blend of Baroque and Classical elements.
The most sacred object in the cathedral is the miracle-working Kazan icon of the Mother of God.
Some churches in St Petersburg were built to commemorate military victories.
In 1777–80 the Chesme Church was put up by Yury Velten. It was dedicated to the Russian sailors who won a victory over the Turkish fleet off Chesme in 1770.
The decor of the church fronts betrays a romantic perception of Oriental architecture mixed with Gothic motifs.
Two majestic regimental cathedrals were designed by Vasily Stasov. The Cathedral of the Transfiguration was erected in

The Chesme Church

The St Prince Vladimir Cathedral

The Cathedral of the Transfiguration

The Cathedral of the Holy Trinity (the Trinity-Izmailovsky Cathedral)

honour of the Preobrazhensky Regiment, the first military unit of this kind in Russia. In 1825 the Baroque building burned down and two years later Stasov renovated it in the Classical style. The cathedral was consecrated on 5 August 1829. In 1832 an unusual fence of captured Turkish cannons was erected around it. Among sacred objects kept in the cathedral are the icon of *The Vernicle* which belonged to Peter the Great and the icon of *The Mother of God of All Sorrows* once owned by Princess Natalia, Peter's sister.

In 1828–35 Stasov's designs were used to put up the large-scale Cathedral of the Holy Trinity (commonly known as the Trinity-Izmailovsky Cathedral) in honour of the Izmailovsky Life Guards Regiment. The enormous building with its formidable shapes and huge blue dome studded with stars is a sort of architectural hymn to military glory.

→
Panoramic view of Vasilyevsky Island

Peterhof

Peterhof is a great palace-and-park complex of the eighteenth and nineteenth centuries, a summer residence of the Russian Emperors.

Perhaps the most brilliant feature of Peterhof is the Lower Park with its three unique cascades, dozens of powerful water jets and miniature palaces — Monplaisir, Marly and the Hermitage. The happy idea to lay a formal park on the shore of the Gulf of Finland as a memorial to Russia's triumph on the sea belonged to Peter the Great himself.

The Great Cascade. Decorative sculpture

Perspective view of the Sea Canal

The Samson Fountain

←

*Panorama of the Great
Palace, the Great Cascade
and the Alley of Fountains*

*The Great Cascade
The Waterfall Staircase*

*The Great Cascade
The East Waterfall
Staircase*

The Roman Fountain

*The Dragon
(Chessboard Hill) Cascade*

The symbol of Peterhof, the *Samson* Fountain, is an allegory of the crucial victory won by the Russian troops over the Swedish army at Poltava in 1709. The Great Cascade, created by the efforts of many architects, includes waterfall stairways, fountains and decorative sculptures.

Compositionally, the Lower Park consists of the three ensembles — the central part with the Great Palace and three cascades, the west section with the Marly Palace, and the Chessboard Hill Cascade.

The gem of Peterhof is Peter's favourite Monplaisir and its garden with fountains including two trick fountains dating back to the Petrine era. The brick masonry of the palace façade, its clear-cut and concise forms and its tent-shaped roof remind us about the Dutch tastes of Peter the Great.

*The **Cloche** Fountain*
Sculpture: Psyche. 1817. A copy
from Antonio Canova's original

The Palace of Monplaisir
*The Monplaisir Garden. The **Sheaf** Fountain*

The Marly complex →

The Great Palace is the crowning element of the Great Cascade and of the entire ensemble of the Lower Park and the Upper Garden. Many outstanding architects contributed to its construction: Johann Braunstein, Jean-Baptiste Le Blond and Niccolo Michetti (1714–24); Rastrelli (1745–55); Yury Velten (1763–80). In 1763 Vallin de la Mothe, using authentic Chinese lacquered panels as models, designed two exotic interiors known as the Chinese Lobbies.

The State Staircase of the Great Palace

The Throne Room

The West Chinese Lobby

The Great Palace. The garden front

Tsarskoye Selo is a real constellation of fine palaces, pavilions and triumphal monuments dating from the eighteenth and nineteenth centuries. This place used to by a royal country residence loved by Catherine I, Elizabeth Petrovna, Catherine the Great, Alexander I and especially by Nicholas II, the last Russian monarch. Tsarskoye Selo is the place where the great poet Alexander Pushkin spent his schooling years. The beginnings of Tsarskoye Selo go back to the rich Finnish farmstead "Saari Moojs". In 1708–24 the Sarskaya estate, turned into Tsarskoye Selo (Tsar's Village), became a residence of Peter the Great's wife, Catherine. A two-storey

The Catherine Palace. The State (Throne) Room

Domes of the palace church

stone palace was built to the design of Johann Braunstein and a regular garden was laid out, thus shaping an estate in the Baroque style. In 1743–51 Savva Chevakinsky and Alexei Kvasov developed the modest structure into an imposing palace by adding a church and service blocks. The palace has acquired a truly regal appearance thanks to the efforts of Francesco Bartolomeo Rastrelli, whose genius has left its imprint everywhere — in the design of the forded fence and gate, in the perfectly ornamented five-domed church and in the sculptural decoration of the fronts.

→
*The south front
of the Catherine Palace*

The Amber Study

The Picture Hall, an interior the decor of which is largely devoted to painting, is characteristic of the first half of the eighteenth century. The powerful decorative effect created by tapestry-like hanging of the canvases combines here with the image of a picture gallery, an indispensable attribute in the home of an enlightened aristocrat during that period.

A veritable gem of the Catherine Palace was the Amber Study which is justly ranked by connoisseurs among "treasures of the world". In 1701–09 G. Wolfram, G. Tousseau and E. Schacht produced, after a design by A. Schlüter, the inlaid amber panels which in 1717 were presented by Friedrich William of Prussia to Peter the Great for the decoration of the Study in his third Winter Palace at St Petersburg. In 1755 Rastrelli designed the Amber Room in the Catherine Palace enriching the panels with Florentine mosaics and sculpture. Plundered by the Nazi soldiers during the Second World War, the amber decoration of the Study has nowadays been almost completely restored.

The Picture Room

The Bedroom of Maria Fiodorovna is one of the most spectacular interiors created by Cameron in the Catherine Palace. The architectural image of this room combined the intimate character of a private apartment with the luxury of a state room. Cameron used for the decor of the Bedroom moulded wall panels executed by Ivan Martos, which allegorically personified joy and happiness of family life. But the most prominent feature of the Bedroom are thin faience columns of the alcove. Lavishly ornamented and emphasized by golden strips and flutes, they seem to have come down from the murals of the Pompeiian villas.

Detail of the Bedroom doors

The Bedroom

The Blue Drawing Room is the central apartment of the north section of the palace which was allotted by Catherine the Great to Grand Duke Pavel Petrovich, the heir to the throne, and his wife Maria Fiodorovna. Catherine the Great commissioned the designing of the heir's apartments, which included such interiors as the Green Dining Room, the Waiters' Room, the Blue Drawing Room, the Blue Chinese Drawing Room, the Bedroom and the Choir Anteroom, to the Scottish architect Charles Cameron, who brilliantly coped with the task. The Blue Drawing Room is one of the most remarkable interiors in the palace created by Cameron in the 1780s. Notable features of this interior are the silk upholstery of its walls adorned with a printed pattern, the artistic paintings of the ceilings and doors as well as the inlaid parquet floor. In all this majestic spectacle free improvisations of motifs borrowed from ancient art can be traced. Set into the moulded frieze with a gilded relief ornament are painted medallions featuring ancient images. The ceiling of the Blue Drawing Room is embellished with decorative painting based on semi-circles, rectangles and squares. Painted within the geometrical figures are mythological scenes and characters. The rich design of the inlaid parquet floor matches the elaborate compositional forms of the painted ceiling. Compositionally linked to the Catherine Palace is Cameron's superb creation — a complex which includes a gallery bearing the architect's name. The Cameron Gallery is a veritable masterpiece of European Classical art. Worthy of particular note is its spiral stairway with giant bronze copies of ancient statues of *Flora* and *Hercules*. The gem of the ensemble is the building

The Catherine Palace. The Blue Drawing Room

The Cameron Gallery

of the Agate Rooms, the walls of which are faced with coloured Urals marble (agate) and jasper and decorated with sculpture. Marble sculptural decoration and unique structures scattered all around both regular and landscaped parts of the Catherine Park lend to it an alive and noble atmosphere. Worthy of particular mention among such structures are the Baroque pavilions — the Hermitage and the Grotto, the monuments of Russian naval glory — the Chesme and Morea Columns and the Kagul Obelisk, as well as the fountain *Girl with a Pitcher* made famous by Pushkin.

Pavlovsk

Pavlovsk is a palace-and-park complex dating from the last quarter of the eighteenth century, a place where the lavishness of interiors did not diminish a lofty atmosphere and majesty was not achieved at the expense of family comfort and friendly communication. Pavlovsk was founded in 1777, when the construction of a small grand ducal palace began on the tract of land allotted to Paul, the heir to the throne, and his consort Maria. In 1780–86 Cameron's designs were used to build a palace on the estate, to lay out a park around it and to put up several pavilions including the Temple of Friendship, the Apollo Colonnade and the Pavilion of the Three Graces. Between 1786 and 1799 Vincenzo Brenna extended the palace and redecorated the state rooms and living apartments. He also designed a number of decorative structures in the park such

The Pavlovsk Palace
View from the Bridge of Centaurs

The Picture Gallery

The Italian Hall

as the Peel Tower, the Theatrical Gate and the Ruin Cascade. In 1802–05, Andrei Voronikhin, Giacomo Quarenghi, Thomas de Thomon, Carlo Rossi and the best Russian sculptors were active at Pavlovsk. The most remarkable interiors in the palace are the Italian and Grecian Halls, the Hall of War, the Picture Gallery and the Rossi Library, which are illustrious examples of a synthesis of architecture, decorative painting and sculpture.

The State Bedroom of Empress Maria Fiodorovna designed by Vincenzo Brenna is notable for the extreme luxury of its decoration. The walls of the room are lined with silk panels painted in bright colours. Their motifs are symbols of idyllic pastoral life at one with nature. The Little Lantern Study, a truly inspired work by Voronikhin, is perceived as an antithesis to the pomposity of the Bedroom. The Pavlovsk Park is the largest among the royal suburban residences. This park, created under the supervision of Pietro Gonzago, is one of the most perfect examples of landscape gardening in the environs of St Petersburg and might be called "a music for the eye".

←The Pavlovsk Palace and the Parade Ground

The State Bedroom

Saint Petersburg

English edition

Ivan Fiodorov Art Publishers, St Petersburg
11 Zvenigorodskaya St, 191119, St Petersburg, Russia

IVAN FIODOROV PRINTING COMPANY, ST PETERSBURG (NO 2271)
PRINTED AND BOUND IN RUSSIA